Spenser Wilkinson

Citizen Soldiers Essays

Towards the Improvement of the Volunteer Force

Spenser Wilkinson

Citizen Soldiers Essays
Towards the Improvement of the Volunteer Force

ISBN/EAN: 9783337131203

Printed in Europe, USA, Canada, Australia, Japan

Cover: Foto ©ninafisch / pixelio.de

More available books at **www.hansebooks.com**

CITIZEN SOLDIERS

ESSAYS

TOWARDS THE IMPROVEMENT OF
THE VOLUNTEER FORCE

BY

SPENSER WILKINSON

SECOND EDITION

LONDON
SWAN SONNENSCHEIN & CO.
PATERNOSTER SQUARE
1894

PREFACE TO THE SECOND EDITION.

IN re-issuing these essays after the lapse of ten years, I have little to add and nothing to unsay. Since 1883, some of the changes I proposed have been made, and others have been caricatured. The standard of shooting required for efficiency has been raised. The drill book has been simplified, and far too frequently altered. The war game has occasionally been practised, and very commonly misapplied. The volunteers have received a great deal more money from Government. Elaborate arrangements have been made for mobilisation, and the equipment has been improved. But the force is still unfit for war; the essentials have been neglected. Exactitude in elementary drill, intelligence and suppleness in skirmishing, have not become common. Ranges are not more numerous, nor more accessible; manœuvre-grounds are as rare as ever. The officers, upon whom everything depends, are little better fitted to lead their troops in a campaign than they were ten years ago. The War Office will not encourage nor permit promotion by results. It has appointed amateur, unpaid, irresponsible brigadiers, and has left the adjutants, who do whatever work of instruction is done, exactly where they were. The consequence is, that the officers as a body have not become tacticians. Many of them, it is true, have passed the examination instituted, at my suggestion, in 1881, but no step has been taken by the War Office to help them beyond this elementary stage. Discipline varies according to the character of commanding officers, and is nowhere remarkable for its excellence.

Meanwhile the progress of Continental armies has been rapid and constant. The French army could afford, without sensibly weakening the defences of France, to detach three or four army corps for the invasion of England. It is still true that "the security of England from invasion rests primarily on the command of the sea." But whereas in 1883 there was, perhaps, no immediate prospect of our losing that command, in 1894 the question is not whether it can be lost, but whether it can be recovered. If a war should now break out, it would begin with a fight for the mastery at sea, in which the numerical odds might easily be against this country. In the event of a naval mishap, the fate of England would rest upon the fighting value of the volunteers; that is, in the main, upon the character and the tactical attainments of the volunteer officers, whom the War Office has neglected, and has befooled with decorations in lieu of the instruction and the responsibility they needed.

The volunteer force is a sham, as every serious volunteer knows. The principal cause of the failure to improve enough—there has been some improvement—is, that the War Office itself is a make-believe, tolerated only because the possibilities of war do not enter as a serious factor into the calculations of British governments.

The volunteer officer, however, need not despair. His instruction, after all, lies in his own hands, and there are better books now to be had than there were ten years ago. By far the best are the German Drill Books for Infantry

PREFACE TO THE SECOND EDITION.

and for Field Artillery, and the German Order of Field Service, of all of which English translations are to be had. The volunteer officer who will make up his mind to train himself by independent study will not find it impossible; and though the vagaries of incompetent ministers of war may often make his task more arduous, he will, by regarding them as the inevitable thorn in the flesh, and complying with all the requirements of discipline, acquire a more steadfast character and a better hold of true principles than by yielding to the temptation to revolt against the constituted authorities.

S. W.

3, Madeira Road,
  Streatham.
May 9th, 1894.

PREFACE.

Many years ago the writer, then an undergraduate at Oxford, was attracted by the spectacle of a continent in arms to seek some explanation of so strange a phenomenon and some insight into the workings of a system perfected with so much energy. To become a volunteer was the necessary complement of the studies thus begun, and the practical experience of Volunteering obtained in conjunction with a diligent reading of modern writers on war, has led to the formation of the views which are now not hastily, and it is hoped, not inopportunely put forward.

There is hardly a fact asserted or an opinion expressed in the following pages which has not formed the subject of repeated discussions with volunteer officers of zeal and experience, and the present publication would not have been ventured upon were it not for the general agreement which exists between the author and many of his brother officers, and, he may perhaps be allowed to add, the success which has attended his first step in the direction of reform, the suggestion of a voluntary examination in tactics.*

At the risk of wearying the general reader, and perhaps of offending the professional soldier, to whom such matters will be familiar, a few suggestions have been made with regard to a mode of study, which may be of use to volunteer officers. They embody lessons learned by the writer from his own reading, and experience gained from the work of the Oxford Kriegsspiel Club during its early years (1876-7), and of the Manchester Tactical Society since its foundation three years ago.

* See Appendix II.

PREFACE.

The essays here collected, excepting only VII. and X., were originally written as occasional articles for the *Manchester Guardian,* and the author's best thanks are due to the editor for his kind permission to reprint them.

The Polygon,
   Ardwick,
      Manchester,
         October 29, 1883.

TABLE OF CONTENTS.

                                                      PAGE.

PREFACE .... iii.

I.—THE VOLUNTEERS AND THE NATION:
    Influence of the volunteer force in producing a feeling of security.—Numerical comparison between the English and foreign armies.—Necessity of a defensive force in addition to the regular army.—Are the volunteers, at present, a satisfactory supplement to our national defences?—The existing shortcomings 9

II.—VOLUNTEER SHOOTING:
    The regulation standard of efficiency governs the whole system.—The regulation standard for shooting.—Explanation of the standard.—Nullity of the results it produces 16

III.—VOLUNTEER SHOOTING—*continued*:
    The importance of accurate shooting at short ranges proved by experience, by authority, and by the nature of the rifle itself.—Changes suggested 24

IV.—VOLUNTEER DRILL:
    Meaning of drill.—Difference between training needed for volunteers and that needed for the line.—Volunteers should perfect themselves in essentials.—What are the essentials?—Uniform attendance required.—How to be obtained 32

V.—VOLUNTEER SKIRMISHING:
    Difference between movements of close and of dispersed order.—Importance of the latter.—Careful training the only means of learning to skirmish. 40

CONTENTS.

VI.—VOLUNTEER OFFICERS:
The ideal volunteer officer.—Training required to produce him.—How that training is acquired abroad.—Commanding officers.................. 49

VII.—THE METHOD OF STUDY (The "War Game"):
Practical suggestions on the study of tactics.—The practice of manœuvres on the map.—The kind of benefit derived from these manœuvres.—Manœuvres in the field with imaginary troops.—The tactical examination........................ 60

VIII.—VOLUNTEER ORGANISATION:
Value of organisation in war.—Want of it in the English system.—System of promotion advocated.—Brigade organisation of the volunteer force.—The Adjutants...................................... 75

IX.—MOBILISATION AND MARCHING:
Mobilisation distinguished from concentration.—Experience shows that mobilisation must be systematised during peace.—Want of a system of mobilisation for the volunteers.—Marching requires practice.—Illustrations from recent campaigns. 82

X.—CONCLUSION:
Answers to the questions raised at the beginning.—The proposed reforms involve no expense.—Importance of the volunteers to the nation, and to the cause of free government. 89

APPENDIX I.—List of works on subjects treated in the text 94

APPENDIX II.—Memorandum on the Tactical Examination 97

I.

THE VOLUNTEERS AND THE NATION.

The security of England from invasion rests primarily on our command of the sea—a command which, fortunately, there is no immediate prospect of our losing. But, like his wiser forefathers, who thought it a good thing to have two strings to their bow, the sensible Englishman of to-day would be very uneasy if he thought we had not ready, in case our first line—the sea—should be forced, a second line in the shape of a defensive army on shore. There is, first, the regular army, then the militia, and then the volunteers. They cost between them over fifteen millions a year, and they ought to give a good account of any invaders. That is what the busy man says to himself; he has no time to look further into the matter, and there the question ends.

But those who have looked into the matter, and who have been able to study not merely what is doing in our own army, but what the Germans have done and what the French are doing, are one and all filled with a profound uneasiness.

In the first place, the mere comparison of numbers is, to say the least, alarming. If we take the most recent available statistics and leave out the forces quartered in Ireland, it appears that the entire force of the three services in Great Britain was at the beginning of the year 1882—regular army, 62,000; army reserve, classes 1 and 2, 34,000; militia, 99,000; volunteers, 200,000; total, 395,000. Compare these numbers with the totals recorded in the history of the Franco-German war (of which a handy summary will be found in *Macmillan's Magazine* for March, 1883.) It appears that no less than 1,146,000 Germans crossed the French frontier, *i.e.*, almost a million more than our militia and regulars together. All the time, too, there were under arms in Germany about 350,000 men, or nearly as many as our own total. The number of French prisoners sent into Germany was 383,000—a figure about equal to that of the whole British army at home, together with the militia and the volunteers.

It is true, no doubt, that the whole invading army was not thrown across the frontier at once, but the speed with which it was made ready is no less startling than its numbers. In the annals of English mobilisation the "quickest time on record" is that of the Egyptian Expedition. The bombardment of Alexandria, from which the preparations may be dated, took place on July 11. The embarkation began on July 30 and continued to August 11—that is to say, a month was required to mobilise a single army corps.

Compare this with the record of 1870. The mobilisation decree was issued at Berlin on the night of July 15, and on July 31 some fifteen army corps, numbering 450,000 men, were massed outside the French frontier. Since this was done, in 1870, the German organisation has been materially improved, and France has put forth enormous energy to create another that shall be its match.

It is not merely in numbers and in the rapidity with which they can be assembled that these armies rival each other. The thorough training of each individual soldier is made a *sine qua non*. He must learn to shoot; he must practise marching; he must be taught how to skirmish; above all, he must have a perfectly clear idea of his particular share in the business of fighting.

It would be easy to present these and similar facts in a more alarming aspect, but perhaps enough has been said to suggest the vital importance alike of the army, the militia, and the volunteers. How great is the share of the volunteers in maintaining the public feeling of security will be evident if we suppose them not to exist. It is impossible to believe that in the absence of such an organisation the public mind could rest content. The army rarely has at home a stronger force than that given above, and this may at any time be urgently needed abroad.

It is therefore essential that there should be always at home and always ready an army capable from its training to face any enemy, and large enough to deal with more than a minute fraction of the immense hosts of our neighbour States. Almost a generation ago it was felt that the militia were insufficient both in numbers and in training for so great a task, and the consciousness of the need produced the volunteer force. At that time the dangers were less than at present. The Prussian army was just beginning its reorganisation, and the French army, which was regarded as the threatening force, was not half as formidable as it is to-day. But there is to-day no uneasiness as to our national defence, because the people of this country trust in the volunteers.

Is this trust based upon knowledge? Are

the volunteers as at present constituted capable of taking their place in the field against European troops? The importance of answering this question correctly we have already tried to show. It will be our business in this and succeeding chapters to furnish our readers with the means of answering it and of forming a reasonable judgment for themselves.

At the outset it may be best to say that the answer suggested will be a negative. We believe that the volunteers are utterly unfit in respect of their training, their equipment, and their organisation to cope with continental soldiers. Those who may draw this conclusion from the evidence produced will find themselves on the horns of a dilemma. Either the volunteer force must be made what it ought to be, or the conscription must be introduced. The conscription, however, is what no one will seriously suggest, so that we are brought face to face with a second question no less important than the first. Is it possible without changing its character so to reform the volunteer service as to give it that efficiency which it does not possess? In dealing with this problem we propose to suggest the reforms from which such a result may be expected.

Let it be said once for all that whatever criticisms may be here expressed upon the system, nothing but praise is deserved by the volunteers as a body. They have freely given time and money and hard work for the country's service. They have made the most of their limited opportunities. They have worked on regardless of popular disfavour, and now that they have won over the public sympathy, they are themselves most alive to their shortcomings and ask only for better opportunities than are at present afforded them. But the standard by which an army must be judged is not the progress it has made considering its opportunities. The only standard is its fitness for war—for war under modern conditions.

Leave out of sight for the moment questions of rest and supply, and take the simplest elements of war. The soldier's every day work is marching, and his occasional but all-important businesses are manœuvring and shooting. The volunteers cannot march. They have never even begun to learn. Here and there a colonel has given his men a day's marching, with excellent results; but the majority of the volunteers have never practised the kind of marching which is required from soldiers in a campaign. Then as to manœuvring. Let anyone who knows the volunteers ascertain what is understood in Austria or Prussia by manœuvring, and then ask himself whether the volunteers can manœuvre. Or, again, ask any wide-awake volunteer officer how many men of his regiment are good shots, and how many can be sure of hitting a target at 500 yards.

The first count, then, of the indictment is that good shooting, ready and steady manœuvring, and campaign marching are the attainments of a small portion only of the volunteers classed by the War Office as efficient. A defect not less grave is the almost entire absence of technical training among the officers, a deficiency which too often becomes more marked as the scale of rank is ascended. And finally, to make confusion worse confounded, there is no higher organisation than the battalion; no known plan of mobilisation; and, apparently, no existing store of equipment for a campaign.

It will be the object of the following chapters to make good this view of the condition of the force, and to show that a slight alteration in the regulations and moderate outlay of money will suffice to effect the much-needed improvement.

II.

VOLUNTEER SHOOTING.

"The volunteers," we have said, "are utterly unfit in respect of their training, their equipment, and their organisation to cope with continental soldiers." We propose in successive chapters to take up in turn the different branches of the soldier's work, and to show in regard to each of them from the best accessible evidence what is the amount of proficiency which the volunteers have acquired. The examination of the facts, while it will show that the volunteers have worked hard under difficulties to attain even their present level, will give a natural opportunity for suggesting the changes by which the difficulties may be removed. The volunteer force has always been specially associated in the public mind with the use of the rifle, and we therefore begin with the subject of volunteer shooting.

A brief preliminary explanation with regard to the pecuniary position of a volunteer corps and the connection between money and efficiency may be welcome to such of our readers as are not volunteers. The Government, which defrays the working expenses of the force, has adopted the principle—sound in itself—of payment by results. Certain requirements are laid down by the authorities the fulfilment of which entitles a volunteer to be classed as " efficient," and the Government grant to each corps is in proportion to the number of its efficient members. This capitation grant of 30s. for each " efficient " member and 50s. extra for each " proficient " officer and sergeant constitutes the income of the corps. Special allowances of smaller amount are given to corps going into camp or attending certain reviews, but the sum received for capitation grants is the fund out of which the corps must pay its way.

Accordingly the first business of a corps is to earn as large a capitation grant as possible— that is, to have as far as may be all its members efficient and all its officers and sergeants proficient. This is a condition without which a corps becomes entangled in hopeless pecuniary difficulties, and we find that regiments of good reputation fulfil it with wonderful success. Thus the 1st and 2nd Manchester Regiments and the Salford had last year between them a total strength of 3,218 members, of whom 3,216 were efficient. It is, then, an excellent consequence of the capitation system that those concerned devote their utmost energy to making their corps efficient in the sense which that word bears in the Queen's Regulations, but there is the further consequence that very little energy is left for anything outside this definition.

The corps is inspected every year. That is another official test which must be prepared for, but beyond securing a high percentage of efficients and a satisfactory inspection the commanding officer cannot aspire. In these two points he feels that his responsibility centres, and all who know the force know what efforts are required to carry them. This being the case, it may fairly be supposed that the regulation definition of efficiency comprises all attainments which the War Office seriously thinks necessary for the force. For whatever is required to become efficient, that, if it be a possible thing, the majority of volunteers will do.

What, then, is the degree of skill in the use of the rifle which entitles a volunteer to earn the capitation grant and to be returned as "efficient?" To answer this question we turn to the Queen's Regulations, which refer us to the form of the efficiency certificate. This form contains two clauses on the subject of shooting, one of which, requiring that a recruit shall have fired ten blank cartridges during his first year, need not detain us, as in the case of others than recruits it may be struck out. In the other clause two alternatives are given, of which the first states that "he fired (20, 40, or 60, as the case may be) rounds of ball cartridge in class firing during the year, and passed into the second class." A note is added to explain that if a volunteer after firing sixty rounds remains in the third class the words "and passed into the second class" are to be struck out.

The classes referred to require a brief elucidation. At the beginning of the volunteer year every volunteer is considered to be in the third class. Whatever his previous experience, he must each year begin the prescribed course of shooting, to advance as far as he can. This official shooting is known as class firing, and must take place under the superintendence of an officer or non-commissioned officer.

The first day's practice consists in firing ten rounds from a distance of 200 yards and ten from a distance of 300 yards at a target measuring six feet by four. The bull's-eye is

12 inches in diameter and the centre three feet, while a hit on any other portion of the target is an outer. Bull's-eye, centre, and outer score respectively 4, 3, and 2; so that to score 40 in 20 shots it is only necessary to hit the target every time, while a miss will be compensated by two centres or a bull's-eye. If the volunteer scores 40 with his 20 shots, he has passed into the second class; if not, he is allowed on a later day a second 20 shots under the same conditions. Even after a second failure he may still try again, but with the sixtieth shot his chance for the year ends.

Referring now to the extract given above from the Regulations, it will be seen that he is equally " efficient " if he scores 40 on his first, second, or third attempt, or if he makes the three attempts without any success whatever. This being the only necessary qualification, it is certain that such skill in shooting as the volunteers possess is due, not to any pressure from above, but to their own enthusiasm. That enthusiasm is guided to a great extent by the Regulations, and it may be well, therefore, to examine them a little further.

Suppose, then, that a volunteer has passed into the second class, has learned to hit a good-sized target 200 or 300 yards away, it might reasonably be supposed that his next stage would be to attain greater accuracy under the same conditions; to make an average of centres instead of an average of outers—in short, to become a steady or even a sure shot at these short ranges. This, however, is not contemplated by the Regulations, which not only do not require at short ranges anything better than an average of outers, but do not even make provision to ensure further practice at these distances, at any rate until the following year, for those who have passed the very lax test described.

Once in the second class the volunteer proceeds to shoot at 500 and 600 yards. These are comparatively difficult ranges, so that unless a man has learned in his third-class practice much more than is necessary to obtain his 40 points he will find it a very easy matter to miss the target altogether. The target, it is true, is larger, and the conditions are relaxed, 30 points or 15 hits out of 20 shots being all that is required. Those few who succeed in this, by which they pass into the first class, go on to 700 and 800 yards, distances at which a slight wind will deflect a bullet several feet to the right or left of the target. There is, it should be said in passing, no better proof of the spirit of volunteers than that a percentage of them persevere in shooting at 800 yards with the Enfield rifle, of which an Ordnance Committee reported twenty years ago that at that range it could not be trusted to make a hit within 3ft. of the point where it ought to hit.

So much, then, as to what the volunteers are obliged to do in the way of shooting, and as to the course in which their zeal is directed whenever they have a mind to do more. It remains to see what is the actual performance. No statistics are published by the War Office to throw light on this point, but General Cameron, who takes the volunteer movement in earnest and does all he can to further its progress, has published the musketry returns for 1881 and 1882 of 68 rifle regiments in the Northern district. As these regiments number over 50,000 men, or more than a third of the whole number of (efficient) rifle volunteers, their returns may be taken as fair evidence with regard to the whole force.

It appears that taking all these regiments together the total number of men who fired in each year was slightly over 50,000. Of these, in 1881, 74 per cent. passed into the second class, 28 per cent. fired in the second class, and

19 per cent. passed into the first class. In 1882 there was, no doubt in response to General Cameron's call for better shooting, a slight improvement, the percentages being—passed into second class, 76 ; fired in the second class, 35 ; and passed into the first class, 22.

To appreciate these figures it is only necessary to translate them into terms expressing the skill acquired, and to say that of the " efficient " volunteers one quarter cannot be depended on to hit at 300 yards a target the size of two tall men abreast. Rather more than a third of the force can just manage this, but attempt no more. Not quite a third try their hand at 500 and 600 yards against a four-men target, and only one-fifth of the efficient volunteers succeed in hitting it three times out of four.

III.

VOLUNTEER SHOOTING—*Continued.*

What the volunteers need, and what it is possible for them to obtain, is really good shooting at short ranges. The great battles that have been fought with the breechloader have all been decided by infantry fire at ranges of three and four hundred yards, while the effects which have been occasionally produced at longer ranges were the result of special circumstances little likely to recur.

The Russians in the early battles of the Turkish war advanced in massive columns, which offered the most favourable possible target. The Turks were in sheltered positions in which they could receive unlimited replenishments of ammunition. Thus they were able by an enormous expenditure of bullets to inflict serious loss on the Russian masses at a considerable distance. But the experience of 1866 and 1870 all goes to confirm the opinion expressed by Von Moltke in 1865 that "under ordinary conditions and in pitched battles the decision is brought about not by the refinements of shooting, but by the fire of great numbers at those ranges where errors in judging distance are immaterial."

On this point there is no difference of opinion between soldiers. General Cameron said in his first circular to the volunteers of this district, " It is good *general* firing all along the line which will carry the day, and a body of troops in which nearly every man is a good average shot would annihilate an opposing force with a much larger proportion of marksmen, but otherwise of indifferent shooting powers." Men who are good shots at long ranges will always be useful, especially as such men are likely also to be good shots at short ranges, but long range shooting can never be more than the accomplishment of the few, and it is a ruinous system to sacrifice the thorough training of the majority for the sake of a small number of crack shots.

The relative value of long and short range shooting will perhaps be made clear by a brief examination of the nature of the rifle and of its bearing on modern warfare. Those of our readers who are volunteers will no doubt pardon our digression into ground so familiar to them.

The peculiar characteristics of the rifle as a

military weapon are accuracy, range, and rapidity of fire. Accuracy is of course a relative term, for no rifle is absolutely accurate in the sense that if it were fired twenty times in precisely the same position the twenty shots would strike precisely the same spot on the target. On the contrary no two shots would be likely to hit the same point, the best rifle in point of accuracy being that which will place the whole twenty nearest together, and of course the shots will be further apart as the distance of the target increases.

The Enfield rifle if fired always in the same position (as may be done from a machine rest) will place its shots on a target 300 yards distant within a circle 12 inches in diameter, which at 500 yards increases to 19 inches. At 500 yards the "mean deviation" of the Martini-Henry is 8 inches, and with better constructed weapons the variation is still further reduced. But even a first rate rifle will give at 1,000 and 1,200 yards a mean deviation of two feet and four feet respectively, so that even under the most favourable conditions the best shot in the world cannot be sure of hitting at that distance an object so small as a single man.

In considering therefore the range of a rifle

the essential thing to know is not how far the bullet can be sent (with modern rifles some three thousand yards), but up to what distance there is a probability of hitting the object aimed at. This probability is affected not merely by the mean deviation just described, but also by the nature of the course taken by the bullet in its flight. This may be illustrated from the shape of a bow bent and strung. If the string be the straight line from the rifleman's eye to the target, the path of the bullet is represented by the curve of the bow, except that the bullet falls more rapidly at the end of its course than it rises at the beginning. In order to make a hit on the minimum target (*i.e.*, a target whose radius is equal to the mean deviation), the string of the bow must be exactly as long as the distance from the rifle to the target, and the figures marked at each line on the back-sight indicate the length which this bow-string will have, if the rifle be fired with the back-sight raised to that line.

Before, therefore, you can hit such a target you must know its distance from you, otherwise your bullet will fly over or fall short of the mark. If a larger target be taken there will of course be a corresponding margin for error.

Take a target 6 feet high, and suppose the direction to be true, so that its width may be neglected. In this case the bullet will hit if the target be anywhere in the part of its path where it is falling from a height of 6 feet to the ground. Where this part of its path will be, and how long it will be, depends on the elevation with which the rifle is fired, *i.e.*, on the adjustment of the back-sight.

The Martini-Henry bullet, if the rifle is aimed at a point 3ft. from the ground and sighted for 400 yards, is 6ft. from the ground at 345 yards, and strikes the ground at 450 yards distance; if the target, then (or the man whom it represents), be between these two points the bullet will hit. The distance therefore must be rightly judged, the margin for error being 105 yards. But as the distance increases this margin diminishes, the bullet falling faster as it goes further. At 500 yards the margin is reduced to 85 yards, and at 600, 700, or 800 yards it drops to 65, 55, and 45 yards respectively. Thus the effect of an error in judging the distance increases with the range, and the difficulty of judging the distance correctly increases at the same time.

Summing up, then, the various factors of the

case, the greatly reduced accuracy of the rifle itself, the smaller apparent size of the target, the rapidly decreasing margin within which a hit is possible, and the difficulties of estimating the distance: it is evident that the effectiveness of shooting must diminish out of all proportion to the increase of range. If in action ten shots are fired to hit one man at 300 yards, it will need, not thirty, but a hundred shots to hit one at 900 yards.

But the overwhelming necessity for first-rate shooting at short ranges is not only a matter of authoritative opinion or of theoretical deduction. It is the basis of training in the Prussian army, which considers that good shooting is its strong point. In Prussia, as in England, there is "class firing" in three classes, though the conditions for passing are much more searching than ours. But the three classes represent, not three different kinds of range, but three degrees of excellence at the same short ranges. A man becomes a first-class shot without ever being tried beyond 300 yards. Yet the Prussian rifle is sighted up to 1,500 yards, and the Prussian officers have made an elaborate science of long-range fire.

The changes in the present system which we

would venture to suggest for the consideration of the volunteers and of the authorities may be stated in a few sentences.

First of all, better and more convenient range accommodation is a necessity ; and if the men are to be really taught and not left to take their chance of learning, shooting galleries in the towns and short ranges in country places must be attached to the headquarters of corps. The galleries need not be long. A man can be taught to hold his rifle steadily, to aim, and to press the trigger gently, quite as easily in a hundred yards as in five hundred.

In the second place, no serious progress will be made until the present scheme of class firing and of " efficiency " has been re-arranged. A recruit ought not to be passed until he has mastered the beginnings of shooting—at any rate the three essentials just mentioned. The standard at present required to pass into the second class might be that for recruits, and a third and second class, again at short ranges, but requiring greater steadiness, might be arranged for drilled men. No man should be " efficient " or earn a capitation grant, who did not pass out of this third class, and a slight increase of the grant might be made for those who passed the higher standard. And all who succeeded in doing so should be encouraged to practice at the longer ranges.

To guard against misapprehension it should be said that we mean by short ranges those at which, if the rifleman aims at the foot of the target, the bullet will not rise in any part of its flight above the head of a man standing upright. With the Martini-Henry this will be the case with all distances up to about 400 yards; and the Martini must at no distant date be the weapon of the volunteers.

IV.

VOLUNTEER DRILL.

THE one military accomplishment which is remarkable in the volunteer force by its absence is drill. The word drill seems nowadays to have two meanings. A company may be said to know its drill if the men understand the meaning of the different words of command, and can go through without a mistake the evolutions contained in the field exercise. This is the point which the better volunteer corps are beginning to attain.

But the old meaning of drill was different. The men of Frederick the Great had not merely learned to go through evolutions; they practised them until every movement was ingrained in their very fibres. Such men do not think when they hear the word of command; the word is given, and the machine moves. A wrong word may be given, and the machine moves in the wrong direction as accurately as ever, but it cannot move except with clockwork precision.

Those men had the kind of drill which the volunteers have not. It is like rowing at

Oxford. The merest freshman can work the oars so as to make the boat go, though he may perhaps catch an occasional crab. But his college takes charge of him, and puts him into a tub to be coached. Many an afternoon he pulls down to Iffley and back, groaning in spirit as he tries to obey the perpetual " Eyes in the boat," " Do keep your back straight," " Elbows well into your sides, and by all that's sacred don't put your oar in so deep." In his third term he has passed all this; he has got a " form "—that is to say, he not only rows in the right way, but he can't row in any other way.

The soldier goes through a similar mill. All the turnings, and half turns, and facings which he practices three times a day will be wanted some day when the bullets will be whistling past. If he has to think then what the word of command means it will be all over with him, so he must be practised till he has got a " form." The volunteer, on the other hand, is always a freshman, or at best has acquired only the slovenly way of doing everything which is known on the river as " bad form."

" But the volunteers," it will be said, " can't drill three times a day, or all the year round. They can't be expected to do what the regulars can." Precisely so. That is the first element of the problem. The volunteers can never have one quarter of the practice of their comrades in the line. For that reason, and for that reason alone, they ought to leave unattempted three-quarters of the work which the linesmen are taught. Indeed if the limited time which the volunteers are able to give were really too short to attain the right kind of drill, the best thing they could do would be to disband. But they give time enough for this and a good deal more, only at present the greater part of it is wasted.

This waste of time, which could be obviated with little trouble and no expense, is due to three causes, viz., the drill-book, the system of inspection, and the rules of "efficiency."

The system of manoeuvres contained in the drill-book is very complicated, more so than that of any first-rate army. All the many movements it comprises the regulars of course can do. They have time enough and to spare. But volunteers also try them all and are perfect at none. It would be far better to leave forty of them alone and practice five till they were done with absolute and infallible precision. A battle may be won with very few evolutions, provided the troops have been drilled into them, but a hundred half-learned movements would be of no avail.

There can be no doubt as to which are the few movements to which the volunteers should confine their attention. They are those which would be wanted in battle, and any officer who has passed in tactics could select them. No new drill-book is required, at least for this object, for a single paragraph in general orders would settle the matter. It would be necessary only to forbid the volunteers to practice any but certain specified movements; or it would perhaps be simpler to say that they should not be inspected except in those movements. For the inspections regulate the practice, and their operation at present is bad.

The principal part of an inspection under the present system is the march past and its preliminaries. The volunteers, that is, are tested by the way in which they perform a manœuvre which was driven off the battle-field for ever by the first French revolution. The "old Dessauer" taught the Prussians to march in column and wheel into line, and with these two evolutions Frederick the Great won his battles. They were the essence of his fighting tactics, and he inspected his troops to see whether they could do the movements which he would make use of in action. We have abolished and almost forgotten his way of fighting, but we have kept up his inspection parades because we have quite forgotton his reason for holding them. It is surely time to return to the spirit of his system, and inspect our volunteers, if not our soldiers, in the modern manœuvres of battle.

The reduction of the number of evolutions is no new proposal. Many years ago, when the volunteers were first forming, Sir Charles Napier advised them to learn not a long course of drill, but just seven things, viz.:—

1. To face right and left at word of command.
2. To march in line and column.
3. To extend and close files as light infantry with supports.
4. To change front in close and extended order.
5. To relieve the skirmishers.
6. To form solid squares and rallying squares.
7. To form an advanced guard.

"These seven things," he wrote, "are all that you require. Do not let anyone persuade you to learn more." His advice is as sound to-day as when it was first given, though perhaps the list of " seven things " would be modified by the experience of recent years.

UNIFORM ATTENDANCE REQUIRED. 37

Another reform is needed besides the adoption of few and simple movements and perfect execution of them. A more uniform attendance at drill must be exacted. At present in good regiments the average attendance of the men is about 20 drills and parades a year. There is no need to increase this average, at any rate until the changes just suggested have been tried. The average, however, is made up not by every man attending 20 times, but by some men putting in 40 and others only nine attendances. These latter comply with the regulations; they do all that is needed for "efficiency," and they are the bane of the service. Whatever care a captain gives to his company he cannot get rid of these nine-drill men, and they turn up on all important occasions and put the whole company out. If the Secretary of State would raise the minimum from nine to 20 attendances per annum, these men would either disappear or improve. The force would lose but slightly in numbers, as the average at present is about the figure proposed; but it would gain immensely in quality, for with a minimum of 20 attendances a more uniform training would be possible.

Suppose there were required fourteen company

and six battalion drills. Arrangements could be made to have for each company say sixteen drills, and for the battalion some eight or nine parades. The narrow margin would compel a regular attendance, and a progressive course of drill could then be undertaken. This end would be further promoted by completing the series of company drills before the commencement of those for the battalion, which, again, would be an immense assistance towards the accuracy of both.

While a simplification of the system of manœuvres and the increase of the minimum number of attendances at drill are pressing necessities, it is also desirable to ensure that every corps has a fit place to drill in. At present there is great diversity in this respect. While one regiment which has been favoured by public liberality or by the generosity of a rich commanding officer has a commodious headquarters and a spacious drill ground, its no less deserving neighbour is without proper housing for its offices and stores, and gets through its drills in a shed no bigger than a schoolroom. In Manchester, for instance, Colonel Bridgford's corps has obtained first-rate accommodation, to defray the cost of which it appeals to the public. The Manchester artillery is even better off, thanks to the foresight and the substantial help of Colonel Peacock. But the 2nd Manchester, which has done as much as either to maintain the good repute of Manchester in the service, and which has the unusual merit of never being in debt, is very seriously hampered by the miserable inadequacy of its present headquarters.

It is not suggested that the War Office should buy ground or build head-quarters for the volunteers, but where it is necessary a little judicious encouragement might be given. At least the War Office might forbid any outlay on reviews or on changes in the pattern of uniforms until the requisite sum had been saved, or even might issue a diminished capitation grant for a year or two, and then hand over the balance as a head-quarters fund. But, one way or another, every corps must be properly lodged. A drill-ground and covered shed, a shooting gallery, and a cheerful head-quarters will more than pay for their cost in the greater efficiency and heightened popularity which they will produce.

V.

VOLUNTEER SKIRMISHING.

THE value of evolutions performed for practice during peace has always depended on their suitability for the existing conditions of war. The spectator at a volunteer review would perhaps do well to remember that the line of quarter-columns in which the troops are drawn up to receive the General, and the mass of quarter-columns in which they execute the second march past, are formations which might still be used in the preliminary stages of an action. The open column, in which the first march past takes place, has long disappeared from the battlefield, while the dispersed order movements of the sham fight which usually end the proceedings should be those which alone can be made use of in battle, and for imperfection in which no other form of perfection can compensate.

The aggressive forces of the French Revolution were opposed in the first instance by armies trained in the school of Frederick the Great. The precision of movement required for his line formations was unattainable by the badly drilled levies of the Republic. Profiting by the experience of the Americans, the French pushed out swarms of sharpshooters to harry the trim ranks of the Germans and to prepare for the charge of a column, whose mass should overcome the resistance of some weak point in the less ponderous line.

An army invariably copies the tactics by which it has been beaten, and Austria, Prussia, and Russia adopted the column formation as the basis of their fighting manœuvres. The English, better armed and perhaps more coolly led, found in the line formation a source of strength rather than of weakness. In the Belgian as in the Spanish theatre of war the French columns were scattered under its superior fire.

During the long peace which followed the fall of Napoleon the armies lived on their traditions. Attention was directed mainly to the precise evolutions of compact bodies, which were relied on for all the decisive moments of an action. Abroad the column, in England the line, commanded the confidence of tacticians, while everywhere the movements of skirmishing were retained as a subordinate and auxiliary system.

Thus two modes of fighting, requiring, as we shall see, two different methods of training, were the legacy of the revolutionary wars. Side by side, with close order, for which, whether its application in line or in column was preferred, the troops were trained by the mechanical process of drill, there existed the system of movement in dispersed order, or, as it used to be called, of skirmishing. Most armies, however, during the long years of peace, fell a prey to routine, and as drill is better adapted than skirmishing to the dormant intellectual activity which is the foundation of routine, the practice of skirmishing was more and more neglected in favour of the mechanical evolutions of masses.

The Prussian army, however, was the exception. A succession of able men presided at its councils, and the value of thoroughly trained skirmishers was never lost sight of. The war of 1864 confirmed the opinions as to the preponderating influence of firing which had led to the adoption of the needle gun. The campaign against Austria proved the value of officers trained to handle small bodies in formations adapted to give the fullest effect to their fire.

But the war of 1870 startled even the Prussians. It taught them on the battlefield the absolute impossibility under fire of any but dispersed order. Masses of troops might be manœuvred and assembled out of range of the enemy's guns and rifles, in the old formations of large columns or of lines, but on the actual battlefield and for fighting purposes the only formations were henceforth those of dispersed order.

The relation of the two systems was reversed. Skirmishing, which had been second, became first, and close order was relegated to a secondary position as the method to be used for preliminary movements. The Prussian drill book was revised so as to give effect to this change. The other Continental Powers wrote their drill books afresh; but in England, though the portions of the drill book dealing with extended order were revised, nothing was done to impress upon the army the fact that the centre of gravity of the system had passed from close order and drill to dispersed order and the practice of skirmishing.

Accordingly in too many cases commanding officers are still moving on the old lines and almost ignore the progress of ideas. The volunteers especially have suffered from this cause. Though in their origin they were thought of as sharpshooters and skirmishers, they have gradually tried to assimilate themselves to the troops of the line, and have in this way acquired, along with a limited proficiency in close order manœuvres, a false conception of the nature and value of dispersed order.

This misunderstanding is the more to be regretted because dispersed order is peculiarly suited to the character of the volunteers and intimately connected with English traditions. For the art of skirmishing was carried to perfection in the English army by the Light Division which the masterly training of Sir John Moore had prepared for the Peninsular war.

The nature of skirmishing differs from the manœuvring of masses as a living thing differs from a machine. In the one case movements are possible only if they are accurate, uniform, and simultaneous. In the other case the harmony is no less complete, but it springs not from uniformity but from the oneness of the guiding impulse. In the one system the letter, in the other the spirit prevails.

The essence of close order is uniformity. The men do not think when they hear the word of command; the word is given and the machine moves. This at any rate is the ideal at which even the volunteers should aim in all their drill evolutions.

But the indispensable basis of skirmishing is precisely that free play of the individual intelligence which must be renounced in the practice of drill. This is no new fangled doctrine, no Prussian invention. Its first and perhaps its best exponents were the light infantry of the Peninsular War. The theory of skirmishing was never better explained than in a pamphlet published some forty years ago by Colonel Gawler, himself, we believe, a Peninsular veteran. Colonel Gawler goes straight to the point by enumerating what he regards as "the essentials of good skirmishing." They are :—

1. Active intelligence.
2. Correct firing.
3. Daring courage.
4. Making the best of cover.
5. Presenting the smallest possible mark to the enemy's fire.
6. Maintaining extension from and dependence on a given file of direction.
7. Preserving a sufficient readiness to resist cavalry.

8. A judicious employment of supports and reserves.

A moment's examination of these essentials, which apply as well to-day as when they were first expounded, will show that they cannot be obtained except by a special training. They imply that every handful of men along the whole front of a battle conforms its conduct to the conditions existing at the particular place where it finds itself. In other words skirmishing is based on the handling of small bodies in accordance with circumstances which can only be judged of on the spot. It involves, therefore, that the company officers shall be trained in the skilful management of clusters of skirmishers, and that they shall be familiar not only with the effects of the weapons used both by themselves and the enemy, but also with the use for offence and defence which may be made of every variety of ground; and this practice and knowledge must be accompanied by a readiness on the part of every officer to take the initiative, that is to say, to make such dispositions as the moment requires, without waiting for orders. This again is only possible to those who know the intentions of their commander, and are able to understand the battle as it goes on. Thus it is clear that the successful conduct of an action in dispersed order makes heavy demands on the previous training both of officers and men.

The volunteers have had the benefit of such training to a very limited extent. The correct handling of small bodies is arrived at by the constant exercise of companies by their own officers. This is a practice by no means common among the volunteers. It is enjoined in the drill book, and its necessity has been repeatedly urged, in the Northern district, by General Cameron. But a variety of hindrances combine to prevent its general adoption. Some corps are restrained by the want of a proper space for drill, some by the indifference of their commanding officers to the new order of ideas, and all alike are hampered by the small number of drills required by regulation for efficiency.

Two simple changes in the existing regulations would probably suffice to make the attainment of good skirmishing possible.

The number of compulsory drills should be increased, as was suggested in the last chapter, and the authorities should strictly insist upon skirmishing as a necessary and essential part of every inspection. A great boon would, moreover, be conferred on the volunteers by the publication of some such simple manual of principles as is contained in the first volume of the French drill book under the title of " Rapport au Ministre."*

---

* The Italian army is provided with an admirable elementary textbook of tactics, published at a price which renders it accessible to every soldier.

VI.

VOLUNTEER OFFICERS.

The unstinted praise which we have accorded to the energy and goodwill of the volunteers as a body is due in its fullest extent to the officers. To a degree which few outsiders can appreciate, they have freely given time and money and hard work to the country's service. No class of men, perhaps, has been more constant in the endeavour to make the most of limited opportunities. Nothing, therefore, could be more out of place in speaking of volunteer officers than unfriendly criticism or a spirit of carping. But the very fact that their opportunities are limited, that perfection is beyond their reach, renders it desirable to be sure that such opportunities as they have are used in the best manner, and that the direction in which they make what progress they can is the right one.

To be perfect, as we know, is an attainment denied to mankind, but still it is useful to have an ideal, or model of perfection, as a guide to our endeavours and as a standard by which we can judge ourselves.

What then is the true ideal for the volunteer officer? How would the perfect volunteer officer, if he existed, differ from the model professional leader of troops? The final cause, the ultimate object of each is the same—to conduct with success against the enemy the body of troops entrusted to his charge. But while the one makes it the business of his life to qualify himself for this difficult duty, the other can prepare for it only during his leisure hours.

Clearly the volunteer officer must leave unattempted a great deal that is done by the professional officer. He must dispense with all superfluous attainments, all the refinements and delicate accomplishments of his art, and confine himself solely to those things which are essential.

The captain of a company for instance does not need to be able to conduct a survey or to draw a map; he can do without any minute knowledge of the construction or repair of firearms, and he may neglect, with no fatal consequences, the intricacies of military law. But he has to lead and control his hundred men through the excitement, the destruction, the apparent confusion of a battle. From him at the critical moments the impulse to action must come; it must be the right impulse, and at the right time; all other impulses he must control and restrain. In a trying crisis the steadiness or panic of his company, perhaps of many other companies, will depend on his coolness or confusion. His men, when their comrades are falling every minute, when exposed for the first time to the terrible shelling of long-range artillery or threatened by the sudden appearance of masses of cavalry, will pay scant heed to the fact that he holds a commission. They will look round for a man—for a cool head and a calm spirit—whose resolve proclaims that he is master of the occasion. Well for the officer if he is that man. In that moment he will learn, once for all, the difference between essentials and superfluities. The one thing needful at such a time is confidence —the confidence on the one hand of the men in their captain, and on the other hand the confidence of the captain in himself.

All this may seem, perhaps, a little wide of the mark in a discussion of the attainments necessary for a volunteer officer, but the fact remains that the excellence of an officer depends far more than we are apt to think upon character. And yet how rarely does a commanding officer, when a young acquaintance is applying for a commission in the corps for which he is responsible, ascertain whether the aspirant has the disposition which will gain the respect of his men, or can acquire the habits of decision that mark the trustworthy leader.

Leaving on one side, however, the question of fitness, which it is enough for the present merely to raise in passing, and returning to the one thing needful, it may safely be said that a capable officer will gain the devotion of his men exactly in proportion as he devotes himself to them. The company officer who throws himself into his work, and treats his men with respect and sympathy will not have to complain, at any rate in the volunteer service, of disrespect or want of enthusiasm.

But if one half the problem is easy of solution the other half is infinitely difficult. To do the right thing at the critical moment, to be decided in the midst of uncertainty—that is an attainment which will not be secured either by the most perfect mastery of drill or the most extensive knowledge of scientific books. The mastery of drill is necessary in order to translate the resolve into definite orders; the knowledge which may be gained from books will be invaluable as a help towards understanding the situation; but the power to decide rightly can be assured only by practice. These are the three points at which every officer must be armed—the acquirements which alone will give to their possessor the self-reliance that will be called for in action.

Here, then, is the sought-for ideal, the officer of the modern battlefield reduced to his simplest terms, the standard or model for the volunteer officer. He is a master of drill; he clearly understands the nature of the operations of war, and he has had practice in making up his mind what to do at a critical moment. It remains to measure by this standard the volunteer officer as he is, and in so far as the actual differs from the ideal, to suggest some of the means by which the difference may be diminished.

The first qualification, a mastery of drill, is possessed by many volunteer officers, but there are also, unfortunately, a great many without it. The only test at present is an examination, conducted partly by means of written questions and answers, partly by means of an actual drill. But the examinations take place only twice in the officer's career, and the laxity with which they are conducted is well known. Moreover, an examination is not the right way either of finding out an officer's merits or of encouraging him to improve.

The real need is not of an examination, but of opportunities and inducements to work. Extended opportunities would result from the alteration we have already suggested in the regulations for "efficiency"—namely that 20 attendances a year should be required, six at battalion and 14 at company drill. This would give, to leave a margin for inevitable absences, some eight or nine battalion parades, and some 16 or 18 drills for each company. The company drills should be handed over to the company officers, who should be responsible for them, and no man should be allowed to drill except with his own company.

But this opening for the action of the company officer ought to be accompanied by the proper encouragement. His chances of promotion must depend, to some extent, on the way in which he does his work. It can hardly be over sanguine to hope that a principle which has at last been adopted in the line battalions will shortly be applied also to the volunteers. But the recognition of merit in the system of promotion can only come when scope has been given for showing it by a revised table of attendances.

A clear understanding of the nature of the operations of war was the second element in our standard. The value of such a knowledge, and the mode of acquiring it, are beginning to be well understood, and it is no longer necessary, as it was a few years ago, to use arguments to prove that other things being equal, the best soldier is he who best understands his business.

But there remains a further qualification. Our ideal officer had been practised " in making up his mind what to do at a critical moment." This practice, the keystone of any true system of military education, is altogether wanting in the volunteer officer's routine, and even in the training of our line officers is treated with astonishing neglect. Peace manœuvres give little opportunity for it. They contain so many suppositions required either for the safety of the men or the prevention of injury to property, that the situations they furnish bear only a distant resemblance to those of actual war. And their expense makes them so infrequent as greatly to reduce their educational value.

In all the reformed armies abroad, two kinds

of study are pursued, having for their object the practice of deciding how to act in various situations. The officer studying alone, when he has once learned the principles upon which the conduct of operations depends, and the nature and use of the different arms, has a simple means of applying his knowledge. He takes up some accurate history of a battle, and, having a good map before him, reads just far enough to understand the situation and the positions of the troops, at least on one side, up to the moment when the commander had to make his dispositions for attack or defence. He then lays aside the book, imagines himself to be the commander, and writes down the orders which he thinks would be the best under the circumstances. Then when he has made up his mind how he would have acted, he returns to his book and finds what was actually done. In this way he can set himself an unlimited number of problems, and always have other solutions than his own with which to compare them. Of late years, indeed, this method has been rendered easier by the publication of collections of such problems,* dealing with situations adapted to the needs of every rank,

* See Appendix I., page 96.

and discussed and solved by officers of acknowledged experience and ability.

A second and even more interesting form of these studies arises where two officers, starting from a situation given them both by a third, who acts as umpire, manœuvre against one another with imaginary forces, or forces represented on the map by movable blocks of metal. This practice known as the *Kriegsspiel*, or war game, has been cultivated in Prussia by three generations of officers. To it in large measure they ascribe their readiness and resources in the field, and its general adoption abroad as an integral part of an officer's education is the best evidence of its value. In England, too, it is not unknown, but the authorised regulations for its conduct are cumbrous and obsolete. Their approaching revision is announced,* and it is to be hoped that a simpler and more modern code of rules will be accompanied by some practical encouragement of the game among the volunteers.

* Since the above was in type, the conclusions of the committee appointed for this purpose have been published. The committee doubts the *tactical* value of practice on the map, and recommends the model instead. The model is undoubtedly good, but before rejecting the map would it not be well to consider how far its usefulness has been crippled by an impracticable code of rules?

In this brief and necessarily fragmentary survey of possibilities, facts, and methods the company officers have been chiefly in view. The field officers and especially the commanding officers are a more difficult and more delicate problem. The efficiency of a corps depends so entirely on the fitness of the commanding officer, and that fitness is so difficult to secure, that a suggestion has in some quarters been made for abolishing the volunteer commanding officers altogether and supplying their places from the line. That suggestion is best met by a plain statement. To abolish the volunteer commanding officer would be to abolish the volunteer force. The reflection which any such proposal would cast upon the officers as a body would be well understood, and the volunteer officer, when he resigns, sacrifices neither his profession nor his living. A similar result, though possibly to a modified extent, may be anticipated from the alternative proposal to replace the commanding officers in the event of active service. It may be doubted whether the volunteer force could be kept together if the existence of such an intention on the part of the War Office was generally suspected.

Yet undoubtedly the commanding officers,

generally speaking, are unequal to the responsible positions which they hold. Many of them, it is true, have a thorough knowledge of drill, and some are excellent organisers. But not one in ten has seriously grappled with the art of war, and it may be questioned whether one in a hundred is looked up to by his captains as a guide and an authority in serious professional study. In short, at no point in the volunteer system is there more pressing need for a new standard than in the qualifications of those who alone are entrusted with authority.

VII.

THE METHOD OF STUDY;

(The "War game.")

The portrait of the volunteer officer drawn in the last chapter may perhaps at first sight seem to represent a high and almost unattainable ideal. But that the standard is in fact within reach of every officer who has the intelligence and education implied by his position, and who is really in earnest, may be proved by a sketch of the method by which it is to be sought. The formation of character, of course, lies outside the scope of this essay, but it should be borne in mind that technical accomplishments are no substitutes for decision and presence of mind.

The beginning, then, of the art of war, is a knowledge of the weapons of offence and defence, that is to say, of the rifle and of the ground. It is not enough that an officer can shoot; he must be master of the value of the arm used collectively; for the firing of a company is in its nature and effects by no means a simple matter. Fortunately the subject has now been fairly worked out, and the "Reglement sur le tir de l'Infanterie," published last year by the French ministry of war, compresses into a brief chapter of singular clearness and precision as much as the company officer requires to know, both of single and collective trajectories, and their relations to the various dispositions of ground.

The use of the ground for protection can only be learned by practice, but if the reader finds in "cover" any mystery or difficulty, let him try a few experiments in the first field next time he goes for a walk with a brother officer. Short of a bowling green there is hardly a field in the country where twenty men cannot be hidden from view or half a dozen sheltered from bullets.

For military studies, however, a different knowledge of ground is necessary, the knowledge of its relation to a map. It is of little use attempting to study tactics without first becoming perfect in reading the map, an accomplishment which is unfortunately far from common. In England no maps are published which give at the same time an accurate and a detailed representation of the undulations of the ground. The one-inch ordnance sheets are on too small a scale for our purpose, and the six-inch sheets are so scantily provided with contours as to admit of no such minute calculation as we require. There is, however, a government survey of Belgium on the scale $\frac{1}{20,000}$, in which every change of level, even of a single metre, is indicated by a contour. If the student will obtain one of these sheets and learn so much of the method of mapmaking* that he can draw a section of the ground represented by it on any imaginary line, he will be in a position to begin with profit his tactical work proper. †

In reading an elementary work on tactics, ‡ it will be found useful to work in company; and if the officers of a regiment will form a club or society to meet regularly for an evening's discussion of chapters studied beforehand, they will

---

* The handbook forming the first volume of Col. Brackenbury's series of textbooks contains all the information needed for this purpose.

† It is constantly necessary in the war game to settle by reference to the map whether bodies of troops at different points are or are not visible to each other. This may be ascertained by drawing a section, but more quickly by the following formula. Let A and B be the positions of the troops, A being the lower point, and let C be the highest point in the intervening ground. Find the products (1) of the horizontal distance A B by the height at C (above A). (2) of the horizontal distance A C by the height at B (above A). If (1) is greater than (2) A is not visible from B. (See Sievert, Einige Hilfsmittel zum Planlesen beim Kriegsspiel. Metz 1875.)

‡ That by Col. Shaw, in Col. Brackenbury's series, is the best in English.

find that a few months of such work will produce not only a familiarity with their subject, but an increase of *esprit de corps* and of friendship which will amply reward the modest demands made upon their leisure time.

The elements of tactics once mastered, the society will be in a position to begin the war game, or, as it should be called, the practice of manœuvres on the map. On this subject one or two suggestions may perhaps prevent misconception, and contribute to the usefulness of the most interesting of all forms of military study. Any officer familiar with the use of the map, and with the principles of tactics as taught in the textbooks and in the drill regulations, is qualified to take part in the game as commander of a small body of troops on one side or the other.

But the office of umpire ought not to be undertaken without much more thorough preparation. In the first place, it is the umpire's business to give the situation in which both sides find themselves at the commencement of operations. This is no easy matter, as it involves a considerable familiarity with the nature of a campaign, and is partly governed by strategical rather than tactical considerations. In every corps, however, there is usually some officer who has taste and leisure for more thorough-going study than the rest. The field officers, in many cases, are in this position, and their rank demands that they should be to some extent the teachers of the company officers. General Hamley's work on "The Operations of War" is not surpassed in interest or in clearness by anything published abroad, and its earlier parts contain all that is needed of the principles of strategy. But an umpire must also be familiar with the details of modern battles; and here the English sources of information are scanty. The examples in "Clery's Tactics" are valuable in the absence of anything better, but really detailed and accurate information must be sought in German military histories.

Of these, by far the most valuable is Kühne's "Kritische und Unkritische Wanderungen über die Gefechtsfelder der Preuszischen Armeen in Böhmen," which describes in detail and with a commentary full of rich suggestion the engagements of Nachod, Trautenau, Skalitz, and Soor. The events of 1870 have thrown too much into the shade the instructive campaign of 1866, and no greater benefit could be conferred on English students than by a faithful translation of Major Kühne's Studies. A companion work which should be read side by side with Kühne is the "Studies in Troop-leading" of General von Verdy du Vernois, of which a moderately faithful translation exists.*

If any officer should be induced to give his spare time for a month or two to the perusal of these works, he will find himself taking a new interest in all his volunteer work, and able to form an independent opinion on much of the military history that comes in his way. But more than that, he will find that in watching a war game he is able to see in his mind's eye the battle going on, and to estimate, if not always rightly, at anyrate reasonably, the chances of success of every movement. In a word, he will find himself qualified to umpire between the opposing sides.

The calculation or estimate of the number of men killed will still be a difficulty. In order to have some guide in this delicate matter—it is precisely the point on which the opposing commanders are most likely to have doubts of his unaided wisdom—he will do well to have recourse to the table of losses in one of the modern

* The "Beitrag zum Kriegsspiel" of Von Verdy may also be read with advantage.

handbooks to the game. The most useful is that of Capt. Naumann, ("Das Regiments-Kriegsspiel,") in which the figures can be read off at once from a scale laid on the map. The scale of course must be accommodated to that of the map used.

These preparations for the war game have been dealt with thus at length because without serious preliminary study it is worse than useless to attempt to play; and though perhaps as here recounted they may seem formidable, they will prove, when undertaken with a good will, to be as simple as they are interesting.

Assuming, then, that in some enthusiastic regiment a number of officers have learned the A B C of tactics, and that one or two have gone a little beyond the modicum required for the examinations, the question will be how to set about a war game. A map must be procured giving on the largest possible scale a suitable space of country, and contoured so as to show with accuracy the minor undulations of ground. The cheapest and the best are those published in Germany for the purpose; that of Königgrätz* is perhaps as good as any, and has the advantage that a facsimile on the scale of $\frac{1}{2500}$ can be

* Berlin: Simon Schropp. On the scale $\frac{1}{1000}$.

procured at a still smaller cost. The large map should be mounted on boards, and the portion to be used laid on the umpire's table.* If possible a room should be set apart for the umpire, and the adjoining rooms assigned one to the combatants of each side.

The umpire has sent, if possible the day before, to each commander a written statement of the forces at his disposal, and their position at the commencement of operations, together with the orders under which he is to act and such information about the enemy as the commander might under the circumstances have obtained. The commanders go to their own rooms, and the umpire then places on the map in the positions selected the pieces representing the troops of each side. These pieces he moves from time to time according to the (written) orders of their commanders, who follow the operations each on his fac-simile map. When troops of either side come within the range of vision of troops of the opposing side, both commanders receive from the umpire a written despatch giving them so much information as could pro-

* The pieces sold by the War Office may be used on this map, the slight difference of scale notwithstanding, provided that the length of columns on the march be measured to the true scale of the map.

bably be gleaned by the troops, or their officers with field glasses.

Where a collision takes place the umpire decides on its result, and of course informs both commanders, always remembering that a commander can only be in one place at a time, and taking care that news from the front only reaches him after there has been time for a galloper to bring it.

The time of course is purely imaginary. If the two sides start ten miles apart, the first move, which can be worked out in a few minutes, may represent an hour of the imaginary battle, so as to bring the infantry on each side three miles nearer the front. But in the critical stages of an action where the skirmishers of both sides are giving and receiving a heavy fire, the losses of a minute may change the situation, and the commanders must be allowed to give orders after each successive minute of the battle, although the umpire may perhaps need ten minutes to work them out. It will be found a good plan to have two assistants for the umpire. They lighten his task by calculating the distances traversed by the troops, moving the pieces, noting the losses, and writing from his dictation the needful despatches.

The umpire should concentrate himself as far as possible on essentials; trying to see not the contours of the map and the blocks of coloured tin, but the actual ground and the troops moving over it, now wearied and out of breath and becoming unmanageable under the enemy's fire, now cool and collected as they wait under good cover for the enemy's advance. And the commanders must do their best to believe that the umpire's decisions are right; that is, that if they had acted in the field as they have done in the game the result would have been that which the umpire announces.

The game over—whenever, that is, the umpire thinks the operations for this time have gone far enough—it will be well for all parties to assemble round his table, and for the combatants in turn to explain what they have tried to do. The umpire may then close the discussion by such remarks as he feels able to make on the events of the game.

Considering the importance attached in Prussia to the practice of these map manœuvres, and the fact that in Austria and in Italy they are obligatory on every officer, there is no need here to dwell on their value. But a word or two on the nature of the benefit to be derived from them may not be out of place.

The knowledge of the rules or principles which should guide a military operation is a different thing from the habit of conducting that operation in accordance with those principles; and it is the habit and not the knowledge of principles that is wanted in the field. Now actual manœuvres are too costly to allow of the officer's acquiring his habits by their means, and the manœuvres on the map are therefore the only practicable method; and the habit is far more difficult to acquire than would appear at first sight. Anyone accustomed to umpire in the war game, or to watch at actual manœuvres, will testify that many an officer who is perfect in the theory of tactics will hesitate and bungle when he has to place outposts across country or make dispositions for a combined march of a dozen miles.

Again, in war the great element is uncertainty. You have reports of the enemy's positions, and you make guesses as to what he is about; but there is too often the painful sense of hitting in the dark. Now this is speedily realised by anyone who sits down to command a detachment in these map manœuvres. You are ordered to defend a convoy moving behind you to the north against an enemy reported to be six miles to the south, and while you place your brigade as you hope across his path, you have a disagreeable feeling that perhaps after all he is marching round your flank. But he appears as you expected in front, his skirmishers stretching over a couple of miles. You feel terribly anxious to reinforce your own thin line. The officers in command at the front send uneasy messages, and it requires all your self-control to refuse and to wait and see what the enemy will do. And then, just as his attack is repulsed and you are congratulating yourself on having made no mistakes this time at any rate, the umpire stops the game. The enemy's cavalry, which you had been expecting on one flank, keeping your own under cover to receive it, has gone off by a side route and captured the convoy.

Situations of this kind constantly occur in war, but success is for those to whom they are familiar, as they will soon become to the officers who cherish *esprit de corps* by professional zeal, and cement their friendships over the study of troop-leading and the practice of imaginary manœuvres.

Manœuvres on the map, however, should not be too exclusively practised. Too much attention cannot be given to actual ground. Not that it is possible to take the men out on every occasion and practice with the company all the situations of war. But the officers who in winter are accustomed to meet for the war game may go out together on a summer afternoon and learn many a lesson. For example, a tract of country having been selected, and each man having his map of it, the umpire may appoint a commander of outposts with half a dozen (imaginary) companies and the rest of the officers at his disposal. The commander, after thinking over the given situation, makes his dispositions, and gives his orders, judging in the first instance by the map. The party then walks over the ground, and places itself in turn in the position of each of the picquets, sentries, and supports. It will be found that no practice tends more than this to accustom the eye to judge of the capacities of ground and of the mode of employing them.*

In concluding the suggestions here made for such of the writer's brother officers as may take

* This practice has been repeatedly undertaken by the members of the Manchester Tactical Society. On one occasion General Cameron, commanding the Northern District, was good enough to superintend and instruct a party at Shap, and it is safe to say that the General and every member of the party looks back with pleasure to an excursion which was as delightful as it was instructive.

an interest in them, it should perhaps be said that nothing is farther from his thoughts than to prescribe a system for the control of professional study. The war game itself, though compulsory elsewhere, has never been so in Prussia, and as the essence of our service is its voluntary nature, so the better training of the officers, necessary as it is, will progress more surely by the energy of individual initiative than under the too zealous guidance either of War Office regulations or of regimental orders. The examination in tactics is not and was never meant to be compulsory.

There will always be good officers whose tastes are athletic rather than studious, and a system which would exclude them would assuredly be injurious. Unfortunately that indefatigable parasite, the army crammer, has already seized upon the volunteer officer and offers him tactics in ten lessons and a handbook to the voluntary examination in forty pages. This unhealthy mode of preparation is perhaps encouraged by the distinction, borrowed from our University system, which has been drawn between those who obtain "honours" and those who are said to have merely obtained a "pass." The examination is entirely honorary, and while it is good to offer a wider scope to the higher ranks, as was done by a recent general order, it seems a pity to brand with a stamp of inferiority work which is in most cases done, and which ought to be encouraged, solely for its own sake.

VIII.

VOLUNTEER ORGANISATION.

A MACHINE, in order to work, requires something more than the perfection of its parts. The parts must be fitted one to another; there must be harmony, cohesion, unity. It is the same with an army. A number of well-trained battalions, each with its complement of qualified officers, by no means constitute the instrument which a general requires in the field. The battalions must be grouped into brigades, the brigades coupled together and associated with corresponding bodies of artillery and cavalry into divisions, and the divisions in turn combined into army corps, before they are ready to operate under the direction of a single mind. Even then long experience is required by the officers commanding these higher units, and by their staffs, and constant working together is needed by the battalions, brigades, and divisions, before the necessary regularity and absence of friction are attained.

Accordingly on the Continent, where a war is seriously regarded as a possible event, every battalion has its permanent place in the system. It belongs to the M brigade of the N division of the X Army Corps. Its commander looks to his brigadier for control and encouragement, and the brigadier and the divisional general in turn are the subordinates of the general commanding the Army Corps. The autumn manœuvres are exercises of divisions and corps as such, and in them the efficiency of the superior officers is tested. Even the Austrians, who have long been content with no higher permanent units than divisions, have at last adoped the Army Corps system as being one of those essentials which it is too late to arrange at the outbreak of war.

In England, however, the permanent organisation of the line regiments into larger units is not practicable. Every battalion in turn has to take a period of service abroad, and the corps organisation is suited only for a service where every battalion has a permanent home. But the local habitation which the line battalion can never possess, is for a volunteer battalion the first condition of its existence, so that no army in the world offers a more favourable field for the higher organisation than the English volunteer service. How much the service suffers from the want of such a system can be seen at any review where half a dozen battalions are assembled.

The suggestion has already been made, with regard to volunteer officers, that increased opportunities for drill and better facilities for study must be accompanied by the proper encouragement. That encouragement can be given only through the due recognition of merit in the method of promotion.

Those who have been tried and found wanting should be passed over, those who have proved their fitness should be promoted in turn according to seniority, and for exceptional men of commanding ability special and extra-regimental avenues of promotion should be kept open.

This system of promotion, of course, implies as a preliminary the increase which we advocate in the minimum number of drills, but it also involves the organisation of permanent brigades. The merit of an officer is tested, not by an examination, but by his work. To see what he has done it is necessary only to see the company or the battalion which he has trained and to see how he handles it. In other words, a sound system of promotion is inseparable from a sound system of inspection.

But who is to be the judge of an officer's work? Where is the authority that can class him for promotion? The commanding officer can scarcely be trusted with this responsibility, at any rate at present, or so long as there is need for a new standard in his own qualifications. The adjutant, no doubt, could give a valuable and perhaps an impartial opinion, but to consult him as the official authority on questions of promotion would be to supersede the commanding officer. Clearly an outside opinion must be taken, and that from some person unquestionably above anyone in the corps itself.

The officer commanding the regimental district naturally occurs as the sought-for authority. A moment's reflection, however, will show that this too is an impracticable suggestion. The district commander is responsible for the depot of a line regiment, for two militia battalions, and sometimes, as in the case of Manchester, for as many as seven volunteer battalions. It is therefore quite impossible that he should have the personal knowledge of every officer, or make the minute inspection of every company which would enable him to report faithfully on the performance of each one.

But if two or three volunteer battalions

were formed into a brigade, with a permanent brigadier and brigade major, those officers would be able to make a thorough inspection of every company, and to acquire a personal knowledge of every officer in their brigade. The reports on the companies would then be made by the brigade staff, jointly with the commanding officer and field officers of the battalion, and there would be an authority capable of assisting the district or divisional commander in inspecting and reporting upon the performance of commanding officers.

If the positions of brigadier and of brigade major in volunteer brigades were occasionally filled by the promotion to them of volunteer officers, there would be at once an inducement which does not now exist for commanding officers to perfect themselves, and an avenue of extra-regimental promotion for the cases of unusual ability to which we have referred. In short, the permanent arrangement of volunteer battalions into brigades, while it is the first step in an organisation which no European army ventures to dispense with, offers at the same time a reasonable solution of the difficult problems of inspection and promotion.

It will be noticed that in the system of which

the outline has now been traced out the adjutants scarcely appear. There are good reasons for supposing that the adjutant is destined to become a very minor functionary in the volunteer service, as he has already become in the line. As soon as the regimental officers have the opportunity and the inducement to instruct their men themselves, there will be left for the adjutant nothing but the instruction of recruits and the duties of secretary to the commanding officer. The main portion of these functions is at present performed by a staff sergeant, and if necessary an excellent adjutant for such purposes could be obtained by giving him a lieutenant's commission.

The present system, by which captains and even majors in line battalions are seconded for five years to act as volunteer adjutants, cannot possibly last. The five years adjutants, many of whom are officers of the best type, are beginning to feel the awkwardness of their position. They have sacrificed for a time their chances of professional distinction without the compensation which would be found in the opportunity of doing good work where they are. In future, really good men will decline to be adjutants, and none but really good men can be of any use as volunteer adjutants. Moreover, the five years system fails to identify the interests of the adjutant with those of his corps, a very serious evil, which is often painfully felt by the regimental officers of volunteer battalions.

IX.

MOBILISATION AND MARCHING.

We have hitherto confined our attention to those deficiencies in the volunteer system which render inadequate and delusive the peace training received by the force. Bad shooting, loose drill, and incompetent officers are defects which at the outbreak of a war it is too late by any possible means to remedy. These failings must be removed by some such changes as have already been suggested before the volunteers can be seriously counted among our available forces. But there are other matters which, though not essential to the effectual training of troops in time of peace, require to be carefully arranged before the commencement of actual hostilities, and which therefore in foreign armies are at all times fully provided for.

As a preliminary to any operations in the field, the troops which it is intended to use must be supplied with all the necessary equipment and munitions of war, and must be assembled at the point from which their united action is to begin. Thus fighting is only the third stage of war; before it come mobilisation and concentration.

There are two ways of dealing with these problems, both of which were exemplified in 1870. In France everything was kept at the central depots, and nothing was settled beforehand; in Germany every detail had been arranged in time of peace, and as far as possible all the stores were kept at the head-quarters of the regiments for which they were destined. The one system resulted in delay, confusion, and defeat; the other in promptness, order, and victory. Since then the German principle has been adopted in other armies, and the rule has been accepted that mobilisation must precede concentration. In other words a regiment must be ready with all its men and all its equipment before it can leave its head-quarters. Experience teaches that those things which are left behind when a regiment starts out from its head-quarters are not likely to be met with before its final return.

The importance of mobilisation will be seen when the term is applied to a volunteer corps. If one of our Manchester battalions were suddenly wanted for service, its commanding officer would find himself troubled by such questions as: Where are my men to get boots, new uniforms, knapsacks, water bottles, and blankets? What are we to do for ammunition wagons and baggage wagons? How are we to get rid of those men who can't stand the fatigue of a campaign?

Clearly it would be advantageous to let all volunteer officers know by a set of concise regulations the method they are expected to follow in mobilisation. There is no need to keep all the equipment in store. It would cost money, which would be better spent on headquarters, drill grounds, and shooting galleries. But the officers ought to know what are the articles they could obtain from Government stores, and for what articles and to what extent they would have to make private contracts and pledge the public credit. In a word, it should be possible for every officer to know what steps he would take to make ready the troops under his command for the order to march.

Concentration, like mobilisation, depends for its success on the arrangements made for it, and in its earlier stages it is an affair of railway transport. But for the final concentration and for all the subsequent operations the troops have to rely on their powers of marching. Here again the volunteers are short of opportunities. The only attempts at marching which have been made since the autumn manœuvres were given up were those from Petersfield to Portsdown Hill and from Three Bridges to Brighton before the last two Easter Monday reviews, and on neither of these occasions were the distances long enough to test the endurance of the men.

Marching is an affair of practice, or, to use a familiar word, of "training," and anyone who has spent a few weeks in a German town knows how it is learned abroad. Once or twice a week the troops are roused before dawn and march in full kit some ten or a dozen miles, returning tired and dust covered to their barracks at the time when the quiet visitor is just turning out for a stroll after breakfast. Something like this Sir Charles Napier advised the volunteers to do, but his advice unfortunately has been forgotten.

In the absence of previous practice men are apt to break down under the constant strain of continuous marches or the unusual exertions of some trying day. What this strain is and how great these exertions may be is easily seen from an example. When the Crown Prince's army in 1870 was on its westward march from the Moselle and the heads of the columns had reached Vitry and Bar-le-Duc, it was discovered by means of a telegram from London that Macmahon was making for Sedan. The army was at once marched off to its right flank upon Sedan, which it reached after nine days' marching, each corps doing a daily average of over thirteen miles.

Thirteen miles for an army corps means twenty for most of the battalions. They must start early from their bivouac to a rendezvous. Then they are all day in a long column, where every check in front may mean a halt, and where the dust and heat make every mile seem a league. In the evening a new bivouac must be found and reached, and then come for the men foraging, cleaning, and cooking; for the officers the next day's orders to receive and to arrange for.

Sometimes the very first days of a campaign bring the heaviest work. In 1866 the Crown Prince's army advanced through the Riesengebirge from Silesia into Bohemia, the 1st Corps taking the most northerly road, that from

Liebau to Trautenau. The day was hot and the march unusually trying, but Trautenau was reached about midday, and the men looked forward to getting something to eat. But the head of the column was suddenly fired upon by an Austrian detachment posted under cover on its flank, and a battle commenced which soon carried them several miles away from the road. When darkness came on the Prussian commander found himself in a critical situation, and ordered a retreat, which of course had to take place by night. The soldiers next morning reached their old bivouacs, after doing a two days' march and a hard-fought battle in the twenty-four hours, and that, be it observed, on an empty stomach.

The absence of a system for mobilising the volunteers and their want of practice in marching are, however, of comparatively small moment. They have been touched upon here not with a view to the suggestion of a method or the advocacy of reforms. The method and the reform which have been suggested consist in attending to essentials and insisting on thoroughness in the indispensable parts of a military training. But it is well, while seeking for improvement on this cautious principle, not to lose sight of elements in the soldier's business beyond those with which volunteers must chiefly be occupied. It is only by looking all round the field that the public can fairly estimate the efficiency of the service, or that the volunteer officer can realise the extent of the responsibility inseparable from his honourable position.

X.

CONCLUSION.

AT the beginning of our inquiry the opinion was expressed that the volunteers are unfit in respect of their training, their equipment, and their organisation to cope with Continental soldiers. If any reader has followed our criticisms thus far he will be prepared for the repetition of that opinion in a form more precisely indicating the essential points of weakness. The men are imperfectly taught to shoot. Their drill is neither thorough nor suitable to the requirements of the time. The officers are almost destitute of the kind of training which would be of service to them in the field, and the organisation fails to meet the requirements either of peace or of war.

Is it possible, then, we asked, without changing its character, so to reform the volunteer service as to give it that efficiency which it does not possess? We have endeavoured in the preceding chapters to show that such reform is not only possible but easy. It remains only to collect in a brief review the principal changes that have been suggested, and to show that they may be effected without any charge on the public purse, and without any but the most insignificant labour on the part of public servants.

The proposal to add to the stringency of that part of the definition of "efficiency" which relates to shooting need not be repeated, for the great advance made in the present year in the opportunities of shooting allowed to the army and in the consequent requirements, proves that in this important matter the value of practice has been recognised. It is, however, to be hoped that in the case of volunteers the compulsory firing will be more exclusively confined to short ranges than has hitherto been the case.

To obtain the necessary improvement in manœuvring power the suggestion was made that the number of compulsory drills in each year should be increased to twenty. Of these the first fourteen should be company drills, each man drilling with the company to which he properly belongs, and no attendance at battalion drill should be allowed to count for efficiency until the fourteen company drills have been completed.

This change, however, will be for good only if accompanied by a system of inspection in essentials and by a simplification of the drill. Pending the appearance of a new drill book, which, perhaps, is hardly likely to be long delayed, it would be sufficient to indicate by an order the movements to which volunteers should confine their practice.

A greater change is that involved in the formation of volunteer brigades, and the conversion of the present adjutants of the corps forming each brigade into a brigadier, a brigade major, and, if necessary, a brigade adjutant. But even this entails no additional expense, while its importance may be judged from the fact that it is apparently the only solution for the difficult problems of organization, inspection, and promotion.

Beyond these alterations in existing regulations and arrangements, we have proposed the preparation of two new official manuals. The first a simple exposition of the modern way of fighting, which may serve to assist the recruit in grasping the nature of his work, and the second a set of instructions for mobilisation.*

* By mobilisation it should be observed is here meant the fitting out of the regiment with its complement of able-bodied trained men, and of clothing, ammunition, stores, and transport, but not the arrangements for concentration, which should of course always be kept secret as long as possible.

So far, then, there is nothing in these changes which need alarm the taxpayer; but the incidental mention of new ranges, shooting galleries, and drill grounds may appear more serious. Of these it is sufficient to say that the need for them, where it exists, is altogether independent of ideas of reform. Those corps that are without ranges or drill grounds must either be provided with them or disappear.

Even supposing, however, that some addition were made to the estimates for the purpose of building shooting galleries and buying open spaces for drill, would not the nation at large be the gainer, quite apart from the military advantages secured? The shooting gallery, after all, is but a kind of gymnasium, and the open space on which in the evening a volunteer corps may be drilled might also be used all day long as a playground. In our large towns, at any rate, such squares as are found now in every Italian city under the name of Piazza D'Armi, would be a veritable boon to the inhabitants, and volunteer officers would do well to add their influence to the public opinion which is already demanding the clearance of here and there a space amid the dark streets and crowded dwellings which are the homes of the men they are proud to command.

But indeed the welfare of the volunteer cannot be separated from that of his fellow-citizens. If he takes holiday awhile from his daily toil to submit himself to discipline, and to give play to noble instincts too much repressed by the conditions of modern life, he is yet a citizen, far other in spirit than the reckless mercenary of the past or the unwilling conscript of less favoured lands.

The English Volunteer represents a forward step in modern civilisation. He has undertaken to solve the problem of combining military organisation and training for national defence with the spirit of international amity and the permanent security of free institutions. The attempt, it is safe to predict, will succeed if it is kept aloof from the associations of political parties, encouraged by an intelligent popular sympathy, and guided by the military authorities in a spirit of adaptability to the requirements of modern war.

APPENDIX I.

The following brief list of books may perhaps be of use :—

HAMLEY: "The Operations of War Explained and Illustrated." *London:* Blackwood.

BLUME, Strategie. *Berlin:* Mittler. (Though highly spoken of in Germany, adds little to what may be learned from Hamley.)

SHAW: "The Elements of Modern Tactics Practically Applied to English Formations." Edited by Lieut.-Colonel Brackenbury. *London:* Kegan Paul & Co.

CLERY: "Minor Tactics." *London:* Kegan Paul, Trench, & Co. (Mainly valuable for its examples, which are, however, in most cases too much compressed.)

"Règlement du 12 Juin, 1875, sur les Manœuvres de l'Infanterie." 1re Partie. Rapport au Ministre. *Paris:* Dumaine. (One of the best summaries of the changes caused by the introduction of breech-loading rifles.)

MECKEL: "Taktik." Erster Theil. "Allgemeine Lehre von der Truppenführung im Felde." *Berlin:* Mittler.

VON VERDY DU VERNOIS: "Studien über Truppen-Führung." Erster Theil. Die Infanterie-Division im Armee-Korps-Verbande. *Berlin:* Mittler.

R. DE BIENSAN: "Conduite d'un Escadron de Contact." *Paris:* Dumaine.

BRIALMONT: "Tactique de Combat des trois Armes." *Paris:* Dumaine. (An excellent example of the method of studying tactics in connection with the nature of the weapons employed.)

"Die Aufgabe unserer Infanterie in Bataillon und Brigade." *Berlin:* Mittler. (A controversial pamphlet, but valuable as showing how much is expected in Prussia from mere drill.)

VON NICKISCH-ROSENEGK. "Studien über Patrouillendienst." *Berlin:* Mittler.

The principal books on the War Game are:—

VON TSCHISCHWITZ: "Anleitung zum Kriegs-Spiel." *Niesse*, 1874. (The Neisse handbook, inferior to Trotha. This, the original of the War Office code, gives the least satisfactory method of all.)

VON TROTHA: "Anleitung zur Darstellung von Gefechtsbildern Mittelst der Kriegs-Spiel-Apparates mit Berücksichtigung der Wirkung der jetzt Gebräuchlichen Waffen und der neuen masse." *Berlin:* Mittler. (Represents the Magdeburg school of players.)

ZIPSER: "Anleitung zur Darstellung militärischer Manöver mit Hilfe des Kriegsspiel-Apparates." *Wien.* Seidel.

MECKEL: "Studien über das Kriegs-Spiel." *Berlin:* Mittler. (The first essay towards the modern method.)

MECKEL: "Anleitung zum Kriegsspiele." *Berlin:* Vossische, Buchhanlung, Strikker.

VON VERDY DU VERNOIS: "Beitrag zum Kriegsspiel." *Berlin:* Mittler. (Goes through a game played on the system of free umpiring, without dice. The work of a master.)

NAUMANN: " Das Regiments-Kreigsspiel." *Berlin:* Mittler. (Requires careful study, but gives a method much simpler and better adapted for self-taught umpires than any other. The 2nd edition is still further simplified.)

MAYER: " Eine Studie über das Kriegsspiel; *Wien:* Verlag des Militar-Wissenschaflichen Vereines." (A valuable study of method in estimating losses.)

" Istruzione per la Manovra Sulla Carta ad uso degli ufficiali dell' esercito Italiano." *Roma:* Carlo Voghera. 1878. (The Italian handbook stating more clearly than any other wherein the value of the game consists.)

Of the collections of problems referred to in the text, the best are those in Von Verdy's Studien, and in the same author's Kriegs-geschichtliche Studien, *Berlin:* Mittler. An excellent series of elementary problems, with solutions and full discussions, was published in the *Allgemeine Illustrirte Militär Zeitung* for 1882 and 1883, and has been republished in two pamphlets under the title, " Strategisch-taktische Aufgaben nebst Lösungen." *Hannover:* Helwingsche Verlagsbuch-handlung. 1883.

APPENDIX II.

The following Memorandum was drawn up by the present writer, and presented, in July, 1881, to Mr. Childers, then Secretary of State for War, by Mr. Summers, M.P. for Stalybridge:—

MEMORANDUM.

"There is a general feeling among those interested in the volunteer force that the weak point is to be found in the officers, and that in two respects—

"1. There is an inadequate supply of fit candidates for commissions.

"2. The officers generally have no knowledge beyond what is to be learnt from the drill books.

"The former of these evils can best be remedied by dealing with the latter, as every step in efficiency increases the popularity of a corps.

"The insufficient theoretical knowledge of the officers is pointed out, e.g., by his Royal Highness the Duke of Connaught, in the report written by him on the corps under his command at the Brighton Review, 1881. His Royal Highness remarks that the officers do not thoroughly appreciate the nature of an attack in dispersed order; in other words, their knowledge of tactics is slight, for the attack in dispersed order is the cardinal point in modern tactics.

"The 'Field Exercise' contains admirable rules for the conduct of such movements, but it is not the purpose of such a manual to expound the various principles which are involved. Such knowledge is pre-supposed; and it is because they are unable to read, as it were, between the lines of the extended order drill that volunteer officers fail to give their men that thorough training in this respect, which is indispensable in modern warfare.

"The remedy suggested is a voluntary examination, of an elementary nature, in the theory of tactics.

"1. A voluntary test is proposed, because any addition to the necessary requirements might deter gentlemen from taking commissions; while, on the other hand, the number of officers really anxious to learn is so great that the mere opportunity of distinguishing themselves will bring out enough to give a tone to the whole body. Moreover, the rivalry between corps will act more healthily than compulsion, and will tend to promote *esprit de corps.*

"2. An examination is suggested, because it involves no addition to the teaching staff of the corps, and allows room for individual judgment in methods of study. It makes no additional regular demand upon the time of the officers.

"3. Such an examination, however, would be of no use unless it be the same for all, and impartial. For this reason it is desirable that it should be held not too often, say once a year, and in London. The expense would be slight, and could, if necessary, be defrayed by charging a small fee from each candidate, as is done in the University examinations.

"4. An examination does more than test; it guides the course of study. This is an additional reason for a central examination, conducted by men of unmistakeable attainments.

"5. The simplest method of guiding the course of study is to prescribe a text-book. Does a suitable one exist?

"It is submitted that the 'Elements of Modern Tactics,' by Major Wilkinson Shaw (Vol. II. of a series for Officers and Non-commissioned Officers of the Auxiliary Forces, prepared under the guidance of Lieut.-Col. C. B. Brackenbury, Superintendent of Garrison Instruction), is admirably fitted for this purpose, at any rate, in the first instance. This book is elementary; it deals with the problems which face the company officer; it is based on a careful study of the best modern writers, and is sufficiently clear and comprehensive.

"6. It is suggested that, if such an examination be established, the names of those officers who have passed it be indicated in some way in the Army List, *e.g.*, by an additional letter after the *p*, which denotes proficiency.

"It is believed that the adoption of these proposals would be a great stimulus to military study amongst volunteer officers, and would materially increase the efficiency of the force."

JAMES F. WILKINSON, Printer, 47, Spring Gardens, Manchester;
and The Gutenberg Works, Pendleton.

www.ingramcontent.com/pod-product-compliance
Lightning Source LLC
Chambersburg PA
CBHW021947160426
43195CB00011B/1252